Midstream Changes

BURPEE'S Farm Annual 1894.

"THE LITTLE KITCHEN FRIEND."

"Burpee's Seeds Grow."

W. ATLEE BURPEE & CO.

PHILADELPHIA, PA.

TRADE WAB MARK.

Midstream Changes

People Who Started Over and Made It Work

by Nathan Aaseng

Lerner Publications Company
Minneapolis

Page 1: Ranch workers at a cattle roundup in 1902 favored Levi's Double X waist overalls, the forerunner of today's blue jeans.

Page 2: The cover from an 1894 Burpee's catalog features vegetables. Today, the W. Atlee Burpee Co. is famous for its flower seeds and bulbs.

Library of Congress Cataloging-in-Publication Data

Aaseng, Nathan.
   Midstream changes : people who started over and made it work /
by Nathan Aaseng.
      p.   cm.
   Includes bibliographical references.
   Summary: Presents the stories of famous people who achieved great
success after changing careers in mid-life.
   ISBN 0-8225-0681-5 (lib. bdg.)
   1. Career changes—Case studies—Juvenile literature. [1. Career
changes. 2. Vocational guidance.] I. Title.
HF5384.A28   1990
331.7′02—dc20   89-37220
                                                             CIP
                                                             AC

Manufactured in the United States of America

1 2 3 4 5 6 7 8 9 10 99 98 97 96 95 94 93 92 91 90

To the Wickmans, past and present

Contents

INTRODUCTION 9

THE UNIFORM OF THE WEST
Levi's 13

THE FACE THAT LAUNCHED A MILLION GAMES
Milton Bradley 23

HIS FORTUNE WAS CHICKEN FEED
Burpee Seeds 31

SEE THE LIGHT
Coleman 37

WOULD YOU BUY A NEW CAR FROM THIS MAN?
Greyhound Lines 43

THE UNBOUGHT BANK
Hilton 51

THE COLONEL'S CHOICE
Kentucky Fried Chicken 59

MAKING UP FOR LOST OPPORTUNITIES
Mary Kay Cosmetics 67

BIBLIOGRAPHY 74

INDEX 75

The Baldwin SD-10 concert grand piano is the choice of more than 300 prominent concert artists and organizations.

Introduction

Dwight Hamilton Baldwin

Y OU DON'T ALWAYS GET WHAT YOU want, even if you are destined to become rich and famous. Sometimes you get *more* than you want!

Take the case of Dwight Baldwin. His goal in life was to become a Presbyterian minister. But the poor health that plagued him throughout his childhood forced him to drop out of college after just one year. Beginning in 1841, Baldwin worked as a music teacher. Students frequently consulted him before buying a piano or organ, and he eventually began to sell instruments for a living. From 1862 until 1889, Baldwin loaded a rented wagon with six reed organs every Monday morning and called on customers until the instruments were sold.

In 1887 Baldwin's main supplier suddenly dropped him as a dealer. He decided to build his own instruments. Baldwin started with a reed organ, and he followed it with a piano in 1890. The moderately priced piano was a success, and Baldwin eventually let others run the business while he spent much of his time from then on working in his church.

While situations forced Baldwin to abandon his original goal, other people choose to abandon their goals. Philip Armour was one such person. When he was 19, he traveled from New York to seek his fortune in the California gold rush. As soon as he got to California, however, he found that his chances of striking gold were not as good as he had expected. Instead he sold mining equipment to other gold seekers until he raised enough money to buy a farm in New York.

On the way back to New York, however, Armour's train stopped in Milwaukee. He took a brief tour of the city and fell in love with it. He stayed in Milwaukee and opened a produce business. Eventually, he invested in a pork-packing company. Within four years, he had organized Armour and Company. By the time of Armour's death in 1901, his business produced nearly $200 million dollars in sales per year.

Some businesspeople who changed careers in midstream achieved their initial business goals but ended up being more famous for something they had not originally intended to do.

Zalmon Simmons is a case in point. He taught

Philip Armour

The first Armour & Co. plant in Milwaukee

school for three years in Kenosha, Wisconsin, then worked at a general store, where he advanced from clerk to owner in less than a year. By the middle of the 1860s, Simmons was president of a telegraph company and a railroad. At the same time, he continued to run his store and was mayor of Kenosha. He hardly needed another enterprise to worry about.

But an inventor who owed Simmons money gave him the patent rights to an invention as payment. Simmons accepted the invention, a woven wire bedspring, even though the inventor admitted that it was too expensive to be practical.

Another inventor showed Simmons how to cut the manufacturing costs, and Simmons began making the bedsprings. They sold reasonably well. He then began to make brass bedsteads—a headboard, frame and footboard—to go with the bedsprings. Simmons's beds became very popular and the business prospered.

Initially, Simmons hadn't expected his business to do so well; neither had Armour, Baldwin, or any of the other people whose stories are told in the following chapters. Each of them tried something else first. If they had been successful and content in their original line of work, we would not be eating Kentucky Fried Chicken, wearing Levi's blue jeans, or staying in Hilton hotels. Here are the stories of some people who changed businesses in midstream—and made the change pay off.

A current Simmons Beautyrest bed set

A drawing of the Levi Strauss & Co.'s overall factory shows hundreds of women sewing jeans in one portion of the building.

The Uniform
of the West

Levi's

THE STORY COMMONLY TOLD ABOUT Levi Strauss is that of a young man arriving in California after a long boat ride from New York. After displaying the line of dry goods, or fabrics, that he had brought to sell to the gold miners, he awaited the verdict from his first customer. An old prospector is said to have inspected the merchandise, mostly canvas for tents and wagons. To Strauss's anguish, the prospector stepped away and shook his head.

"You should've brought pants," he told Strauss. Pants were wearing out fast among the prospectors, who kneeled on rocks while panning for gold. Pants had a far better chance of selling than Strauss's tent canvas. Heeding the advice, so the story goes, Levi Strauss took the canvas to a tailor to make pants.

At least one historical researcher has concluded that the legend is merely an old miners' tale. That reasearcher says that Strauss actually sold his line of dry goods quite successfully when he arrived in California, and that it was not until nearly 20 years later that he began manufacturing pants in San Francisco.

All sources agree, however, that when Strauss headed for the West Coast, he had no inkling that his name would ever be associated with pants. It took a midstream change for him to make the blue jeans that would influence the way people dress around the world for well over a century later.

Levi Strauss was born in Bavaria in 1829. Two years after his father's death in 1845, 18-year-old Levi immigrated to the United States with the rest of his family. He had two brothers who were following in their father's footsteps as dry-goods merchants in New York City. But Levi went to Louisville, Kentucky, where he supported himself as a traveling peddler. He sold goods provided by his brothers.

Strauss arrived in California aboard a ship that came from New York via Cape Horn in 1853. A brother-in-law, David Stern, had sent word that a fortune could be made by supplying California gold miners with everyday necessities. When Strauss set out for San Francisco, he was carrying a load of canvas and fine cloth from his brothers' New York store.

Levi Strauss & Co. set up its store at 14-16 Battery Street in San Francisco. The company still operates from San Francisco.

In the time that had passed since the gold strike in 1849, San Francisco had been transformed from a small town to a sprawling, lawless, base camp for thousands of gold prospectors. By the mid-1860s, Levi Strauss & Co., which was formed in 1850 by David Stern and was later renamed after Levi Strauss, had grown into a prosperous dry-goods business. Among other goods, Strauss sold pants that were manufactured under the Levi name by a New York plant. The company might have continued to prosper simply as a dry-goods outlet were it not for an unusual letter that the company received from a tailor in Reno, Nevada. Jacob Davis,

Jacob W. Davis

Levi Strauss

Competition is one of the basic features of the U.S. business system. **Competition** means trying to get something that others are also trying to get. Competition in business can occur in many ways. Producers compete for the best raw materials. Businesses compete with each other for the most customers. One way to do this is by selling a product at a lower price than other manufacturers. Another way is to provide some other kind of advantage. Davis's advantage was that he could offer a pair of pants that was more durable, or would last longer, than those made by his competitors.

an immigrant from Latvia, had frequently heard complaints from outdoor workers that their clothes didn't hold up against harsh treatment. The most common complaint was that the pockets ripped at the seams. Jacob Davis had tried repeatedly, without success, to find a better method of stitching pockets.

In December of 1870, Davis had accepted an order for a pair of extremely durable pants for a woodcutter. He used the heaviest cloth he could find, duck twill, a material he used to make wagon covers, tents, and horse blankets. When he finished sewing the pants, Davis happened to notice some rivets that he had been using to fasten leather straps onto horse blankets. That gave him the idea to fasten rivets to the corners of the pockets to keep them from tearing. The heavy pants with rivets worked very well, and before long the tailor was swamped by requests for riveted pants.

Davis saw that he had stumbled upon an extremely successful idea. He also knew, though, that he needed help. Without the funds to apply for patent protection, Davis knew his competitors would soon begin making and selling their own riveted pants. The only way he could think of to head off the imitators was to enlist the aid of a wealthy ally. Levi Strauss & Co., the supplier of his material, had always treated him fairly. So, with the help of a friend who knew the English language better than he did, Davis wrote to the company. He offered to give a portion of the patent rights to Levi Strauss if the company would apply for the patent. Levi Strauss immediately saw the sales potential for Davis's pants. After applying for a patent and sending in three amendments, or changes, the company lawyers finally obtained a patent for Davis on May 20, 1873. Davis continued to sew the pants on his own while waiting for the patent. When the patent was assured, he moved to San Francisco to work with Levi Strauss. With Davis employed on the manufacturing end, Levi Strauss now owned a pants-making plant.

One of the shipments Strauss received from New York was a new kind of heavy cloth. Originating in the town of Nîmes, France, it was commonly known as *serge de Nîmes*. After a time, the name was shortened to *denim*. Davis had made some pants with the material. He usually charged $2.50 for the denim pants and $3 for the canvas pants. The blue cloth proved to be much more comfortable than canvas, and Strauss began using it exclusively.

It was this version of pants, which Strauss called the "501 Double X blue denim waist overall," that established Levi's pants as the uniform of the West. A shrewd man when it came to merchandising, Strauss also added a trademark patch and a unique pocket stitch. The patch showed two horses pulling on a pair of Levi's in opposite directions, in an unsuccessful effort to tear them. Levi Strauss also offered to replace, free of charge, any pants that ripped.

A **patent** is the exclusive right to own, use, and dispose of an invention. The U.S. Patent Office issues more than 1,200 patents each week. Patents for inventions are granted to the owner for 17 years; then the patent expires.

Opposite: In about 1919 a Levi Strauss & Co. factory worker sewed for the Koverall division that specialized in clothes for children.

The Levi patch and the familiar Levi pocket stitch are trademarks. A **trademark** is a distinctive, legally protected symbol, title, or design used by a company to distinguish its products from those of other companies. Many companies spend a lot of money protecting their trademarks.

The trademark patch that Strauss added in the 1800s is still used today.

Levi's pants sold better than Strauss had expected. They were worn not only by miners, but by just about anyone who worked in a rugged outdoor profession. Farmers, cowboys, oil drillers, and railroad men began to buy them.

Strauss never married, but he liked to involve family in his business. He had worked with his sister and brother-in-law to open his first shop. Later, a large assortment of brothers, nephews, and in-laws joined the partnership.

By the turn of the century, Levi Strauss & Co. had carved out a small empire. But even though the company had made and sold nearly 100 million pairs since 1873, blue jeans were considered a specialty item of the West. Sales never topped more than a few million dollars in a year. After World War I, business was extremely slow. Levi had higher production costs than its competitors, and the company was almost shut down.

Some fashion experts have credited dude ranches, vacation resorts that were popular in the 1930s, with making blue jeans an almost universal garment. Easterners wondering what to wear when vacationing at such places were told that blue jeans were the best bet. Gradually it became more acceptable to wear blue jeans in places other than farms and ranches.

Still, it was not until 1953, more than 100 years after its founding, that Levi Strauss & Co. began manufacturing its own jeans in the East. Then, as

It costs money to make products. Businesses have to pay for the raw materials that are used to make their products. They have to pay workers involved in production. They have to pay for energy used in manufacturing. All of those expenses make up the **production costs**. After World War I, prices for the cotton used in making denim went down drastically. Without realizing that prices would fall, Levi Strauss & Co. had bought a large supply of cotton at the old, higher price. So, while Levi's competitors were able to make blue jeans with the cheaper cotton and charge less for the product, Levi was using its higher-priced cotton and had to charge more for its jeans.

A business with two or more owners, or partners, like the business Levi Strauss started with his relatives, is called a **partnership**. A business owned by just one person is called a **sole proprietorship**. Large companies with many owners are called **corporations**. Although the corporation has become the major form of business in the U.S.—providing the most jobs and generating the most income —most businesses are still sole proprietorships.

blue jeans became more and more popular with a large number of children and teenagers during the baby-boom era, sales soared. Those "pants of Levi's" spread to countries all over the world and infiltrated all corners of the fashion world, including the expensive designer market. Levi Strauss & Co. has become a billion-dollar corporation. But even more astounding is the influence that the fashion innovation by Davis and Strauss has had on Western culture. The 501 blue jeans that were introduced more than 110 years ago are still made, virtually unchanged from the original jeans. In 1971 blue jeans were singled out by the Coty Awards as the United States's outstanding contribution to international fashion. Not a bad accomplishment for a man who saw himself simply as a salesman.

The First
MILTON BRADLEY
LITHOGRAPH
PRESS
1860

The Face That Launched a Million Games

Milton Bradley

The word **investment** is used to describe the act of putting out money or something else of value for another thing of value, perhaps machinery or a part ownership in a company. People make investments with the expectation that they will get the money back with a little extra if the venture in which they invested is successful. In Milton Bradley's case, he bought the press thinking he would be able to make money by printing things for other people.

The word **manufacture** refers to the making of articles by hand or with machines.

ANYONE WHO HAS ENJOYED PLAYing games manufactured by the Milton Bradley Company owes a note of thanks to Abraham Lincoln. The company was founded after an incident involving an 11-year-old girl and the 16th president of the United States—an incident that resulted in the near-ruin of a Massachusetts printer. That printer, Milton Bradley, needed to salvage his investment in printing equipment, so he turned out a board game.

Milton Bradley was born in Vienna, Maine, in 1836, a descendant of some of the first European settlers to arrive in the New World. Milton's father was a country merchant who brought a new industry into Maine—the manufacture of potato starch. His expectations of prosperity were crushed, however, by a sudden outbreak of potato rot. Milton's father lost everything, and in 1847, the family moved to Lowell, Massachusetts, to start over.

Because the family was poor, 10-year-old Milton was put to work delivering packages for a dry-goods store. He continued to attend school, though, and graduated from high school in 1854. Still living with his parents, he found work in the office of a draftsman and patent agent. His job was to make detailed drawings and copy the specifications of the inventions to be patented. He worked until he saved enough money to enroll at Lawrence Scientific School in Cambridge in 1855.

In 1856 the family moved to Hartford, Connecticut, and Milton quit school and went with them. He could find no work in his new town. He moved to Springfield, Massachusetts, where he was hired as a draftsman for the firm of Blanchard & Kimball. This locomotive manufacturer went out of business in 1858.

This time Bradley decided to take advantage of his work experience, and he set himself up in business as a draftsman specializing in patent applications. Eventually, he branched into other areas of drafting and even made the drawings for a private car ordered by the khedive, or ruler, of Egypt.

Bradley's life was still far from settled, however. In 1859 he became interested in lithography, a printing process. After attending a school in Providence, Rhode Island, Bradley returned to

Milton Bradley worked as a drafts-man in the 1850s before buying a printing press that would lead him into a career of manufacturing games.

Springfield in 1860, bought a press, and began searching for customers.

His first important printing job was a portrait of Abraham Lincoln. A local newspaperman had brought back the portrait from the Republican nominating convention. Bradley made up hundreds of thousands of prints of the Lincoln photograph to sell. His instincts were correct, as Lincoln was elected president. But at the same time, Bradley had an incredible stroke of bad luck.

The original cause of his trouble was a letter

When a previously clean-shaven Abraham Lincoln decided to grow a beard, Bradley had to throw away his outdated prints of the president.

written by an 11-year-old girl from Westfield, New York, named Grace Bedell. She wrote Lincoln a letter advising him to grow whiskers on his cheeks, because then all the ladies would like him and would get their husbands to vote for him.

Despite the unlikely reasoning behind the girl's suggestion, an amused Lincoln wrote back, kindly thanking her for her concern. In his response, he seemed to dismiss the proposal, but a short time later Lincoln was sporting a beard.

Lincoln's sudden decision to grow a beard was a crippling blow to Bradley's new lithography business. After investing heavily in prints of a smooth-shaven Lincoln, Bradley now had a picture that was obviously out-of-date. There was nothing to do but destroy the pictures.

His prospects now bleak, Bradley turned to friends for consolation. During one visit, he and a friend played a game called The Mansion of Happiness. Someone suggested that Bradley might be able to use his presses to print a similar game.

Bradley followed through on the idea and, borrowing some concepts from The Mansion of

The Checkered Game of Life helped Bradley salvage his printing business.

Top left: In the 1860s, Bradley's company occupied one part of a building in Springfield, Massachusetts. Top right: Well before the turn of the century, Milton Bradley Company had built a large plant for manufacturing games. Bottom: The Milton Bradley Company operates out of a building in East Longmeadow, Massachusetts.

Happiness, developed a game that he called The Checkered Game of Life. The object of the game was to accumulate points by having a game piece land on favorable squares labeled "Truth" and other virtues, while avoiding those spaces marked with "Idleness" and so on.

Bradley then took to the road, and traveling up and down New England, sold 45,000 copies of the game in his first year. His business now seemed solid, but he had learned his lesson about putting all his eggs in one basket. Bradley's lithography shop continued to make three lines of products: basic lithographic prints, educational materials (Bradley was heavily involved in promoting the idea of kindergartens in the United States), and games.

In 1864 Bradley's business was doing so well that he and two partners organized Milton Bradley & Company. By 1870 his games division was outperforming the other divisions, and he built a separate building strictly for games manufacturing. In 1878 the business was renamed Milton Bradley Company.

In the end, Bradley emerged from his catastrophe in far better shape than he could have dreamed. Because of an unlikely chain of events that forced its founder into the games business, Milton Bradley Company became the largest game manufacturer in the country, making jigsaw puzzles and games such as Life®, Stratego®, Chutes and Ladders®, Candyland®, Battleship®, and Twister®.

Businesses that manufacture different products are said to have **lines of products**. Bradley didn't simply manufacture one product; he made several products. By expanding his line of products, he made sure he wasn't relying solely on the success of one portion of his business.

Candyland® is one of several Milton Bradley games.

In 1894 Burpee's emphasis was on livestock and poultry. Later, the company shifted its emphasis to flower and vegetable supplies.

His Fortune
Was Chicken Feed

Burpee Seeds

Flowers from a Burpee catalog

IN 1872 AN ENGLISH GENTLEMAN VISIT-ing in New York City traveled by train to Philadelphia, Pennsylvania, to meet with a poultry breeder he knew only from exchanging letters. Philadelphia was the home of Washington Atlee Burpee, respected by the Englishman for his careful research and scholarly reports on poultry breeding.

When the man arrived at the Philadelphia train station, he was greeted by a 14-year-old boy. Thinking the boy had been assigned to meet him and escort him to the poultry expert's home, the traveler politely asked the lad's name. The answer gave the Englishman a shock: W. Atlee Burpee! The W. Atlee Burpee.

The 14-year-old Burpee was already an expert on chickens, turkeys, and pigeons. He had every reason to expect that his wealth of knowledge would bring him success in the poultry business.

As fate would have it, however, Burpee never did become successful in the animal-breeding business. He had to turn his attention to the plant world before he found a profitable outlet for his talents.

W. Atlee Burpee was born in 1858, in Sheffield, New Brunswick, Canada. His deep interest in science surprised no one. His father and grandfather, after all, were medical doctors. Science obviously ran in the family.

As a young boy, Burpee began raising pigeons, geese, turkeys, and chickens. An extremely quick learner, he began publishing articles in trade journals. By the time he was 17, he was selling pedigreed poultry as breeding stock from his parents' home.

Burpee's father considered all the activity to be nothing more than useful preparation for the boy's real career. There was no arguing when he insisted that his son carry on the family tradition and attend medical school. He began his medical training at the University of Pennsylvania in 1875. But Burpee did not have the personality to deal constantly with hurt and suffering people, and he quit in his second year. In 1876 he went back to his main interest, poultry breeding. A wealthy Philadelphia acquaintance had invested $5,000 to put Burpee in business. The new company bred and sold top-quality livestock as well as poultry.

Magazines or newspapers that contain topics of interest to a particular industry or profession are called **trade journals**. People usually subscribe to trade journals so they can keep up with new developments in their area of business.

A retail establishment, or store, that sells its goods through the postal system is called a **mail-order business**.

W. Atlee Burpee

A **premium** is a gift offered to the consumer (the person who buys a product) as an incentive to buy a specific good—if the customer buys the product, he or she receives the premium. Premiums are not usually related to the product being sold.

The venture lost $3,500 in its first year, however. Money worries led to arguments between Burpee and his backer until Burpee pulled out of the business. His father, who had resigned himself to his son's career choice—poultry and livestock breeding rather than medicine—then loaned him the money to start his own business. In 1878 the 20-year-old opened a mail-order business called W. Atlee Burpee & Company. He published a catalog from which customers could order pedigreed poultry and livestock. To make things as convenient as possible for his customers, he also offered several varieties of the seeds from which his customers could grow feed for the animals.

Burpee's luck selling purebred animals was little better than it had been before, and he began to realize that he could not depend on the business for a living. Selling seeds, however, was much more profitable. There were far more people willing to buy garden seeds than people willing to buy purebred livestock. To expand the seed portion of the business, Burpee's 1880 catalog listed tomato and cucumber seeds at a discount price, along with the usual livestock section. In order to push sales, he offered premiums to customers who found new customers for him. At one point, he offered a free sewing maching to anyone who sold $75 worth of his seeds.

While Burpee's emphasis had begun to shift to plants, his fascination for top-of-the-line products never wavered. If he was going to sell seeds, they would be the finest seeds that humans could develop. Each summer he traveled for three months in Europe, scouting for the best seed varieties that could be found there.

In 1888 Burpee set up an experimental station in Doylestown, Pennsylvania. There he could test the seeds he brought back from Europe and compare them with other varieties. Eventually, he was able to develop some of his own improved varieties. His catalogs grew to more than 200 pages, filled with mouth-watering pictures, descriptions, and claims of superior seeds.

At the same time, Burpee won customer trust with his unshakable honesty. In 1914 he put a picture of one of his favorite varieties, the "Matchless Tomato," on the cover of the catalog. When the proofs of the picture came out, he was horrified to find that the tomato was depicted as being bigger than it really was. By then it was too late to change the covers. Burpee insisted on inserting a very visible apology in the catalog telling customers that they should not expect the tomato to grow that large. Customers appreciated Burpee's candor. The company even received letters from gardeners all over the country who boasted that they had grown tomatoes as large as or larger than those shown in the faulty picture.

During the course of his research, Burpee introduced several varieties of vegetables to the

The Burpee seed house at Doylestown, Pennsylvania

By growing plants and flowers on an experimental station, researchers at Burpee Seeds were able to learn more about the products they sold. In a process called **research and development**, many companies conduct experiments to create new products or improve existing products. **Research** is investigation aimed at discovering new scientific knowledge. **Development** is the attempt to use new knowledge to make useful products or processes.

The W. Atlee Burpee Co. has its headquarters in Warminster, Pennsylvania.

United States, including Iceberg lettuce (discovered in 1894), Golden Bantam corn (1902), and Bush Lima beans (1907). Yet, he never gave up completely on his animal breeding. Until his death in 1915, every Burpee catalog included a livestock section. Had selling livestock ever made money for him, we might well be without some of the more popular varieties of vegetables, flowers, and fruits in the world today.

The Coleman Arc Lantern, which Coleman began manufacturing in 1903, was the first product put out by the company.

See the Light

Coleman

Hardly anyone goes camping, picnicking, or backpacking these days without some help from William Coleman. The Coleman name is stamped on coolers, camp stoves, lanterns, tents, thermos bottles, and many other popular camping supplies. But Coleman's association with camping equipment was not the career he originally had in mind. He was a teacher for five years before enrolling in law school. When he ran out of money after two years of law school, he began selling typewriters door-to-door to fund the rest of his education. Then one night, while he was carrying his typewriters around a small town in Alabama, he saw a bright light that would change his life.

William Coleman was born in New York during 1870. When he was nine months old, his parents moved the family to Kansas. There Coleman eventually enrolled at the University of Kansas Law School. His studies were hampered by two handicaps: poor eyesight and little money. Because of the first handicap, he found it difficult to read in anything less than broad daylight. He overcame this problem by having friends read his textbooks aloud.

The money problem proved to be tougher. Coleman battled it as long as he could, surviving for months on a diet of canned tomatoes, stale bread, and brown sugar. But by his final year of law school, 1899, he had exhausted his funds. To raise the money he needed to finish his studies, he decided to take a year off to work as a traveling typewriter salesman.

The work was difficult, the conditions harsh, and the earnings meager in the era before affordable automobiles. One night as Coleman slogged along a muddy road in a small Alabama town, he was dazzled by a brilliant white light. When he got to the light, he discovered it was coming from a gasoline lamp in the window of a drugstore.

William C. Coleman

Unlike other lamps he had seen, this one glowed so brightly that he could read by its light even with his eye problems. The lamp, which had been manufactured in Memphis, Tennessee, also seemed cleaner and more efficient than oil or kerosene lamps. Coleman had no doubt that the product would sell well in the many rural areas of the United States that did not have electricity.

Many companies divide their market into **sales territories**. Each salesperson is given a specific territory, or geographic area, in which to sell the company's product. Usually, only one salesperson is assigned to a territory. By dividing its market into territories, a company can make sure all areas are represented, and that there is no competition between its salespeople for specific customers.

The **distributing company** that Coleman dealt with was a business set up to sell goods (gasoline lamps) to customers through its salespeople. Distributing companies also sell goods to retail stores.

Before he left town, Coleman learned all he could from the store owner about the lamps, the company that made them, and the salesman who had sold this one. By the time he left the town, Coleman had decided to switch to selling gasoline lamps. He eventually caught up with the lamp salesman in Missouri a month later. After talking with the man for a while, he was offered a job selling lamps. He turned it down at first, because he thought the distributor's way of dividing sales territories was illegal. A couple of days later, however, the distributing company convinced him that it was doing nothing illegal, and he took the job.

On Coleman's first sales trip, in the town of Kingfisher, Oklahoma, he almost lost his enthusiasm selling just two lamps in a week. It had been his bad luck to start in a town that had already been visited by a gasoline-lamp salesman. Within days after the other salesman had left with the townspeople's money, the lamps had become clogged with carbon. It was a common problem with many early gasoline lamps, and these salesmen left a trail of suspicion wherever they went.

With no hope of selling to the people of Kingfisher, Coleman was about to try another town when he thought of a new plan. He offered to rent out the lamps for one dollar a week. If anything went wrong with the lamps, customers would not have to pay. Within a few days of announcing his new plan, Coleman was able to rent out 100 lamps.

After enjoying similar successes in other rural areas, Coleman managed to break into cities as well. After he pointed out that the gasoline lamp was many times more efficient than the type of light bulbs in use then, urban dwellers also began placing orders for lamps to rent.

Things were going so well that Coleman stayed in the lamp business and forgot about law school. In 1903 he bought the patent rights to the product from the supplier and manufactured it as the Coleman Arc Lamp. Many more uses were developed for the lamps, including lighting areas for large gatherings, such as fairs. Coleman lamps also provided light for the first nighttime college football game, Fairmont College (now Wichita State) versus

An inventor may sell or give away **patent rights** to his or her product. After securing a patent, an inventor may allow another person or business to manufacture the product under the same or a different name. Depending on the actual agreement, the inventor may be entitled to flat fee and a share of the profits on that product.

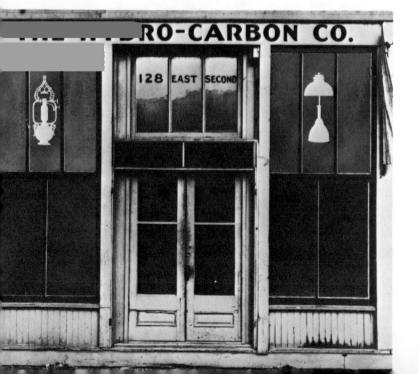

Coleman set up the Hydro-Carbon Co. to manufacture the Coleman Arc Lamp and other Coleman products.

Cooper College, in 1905. Because customers were still leery of gasoline lamp dealers, it was several years before Coleman could discontinue renting and begin selling the lamps outright.

As a businessman, Coleman showed an ability to make the best of bad situations—and he had not seen the last of them. After a period of steady growth, improvements in electric light bulbs began to eat into the company's gasoline-lamp sales. This trend was speeded up when President Franklin Roosevelt encouraged electric power for rural areas.

Companies or individuals go into **bankruptcy** when they cannot pay their debts. You are in **debt** if you owe someone something. Debt is an obligation to pay something.

Whenever bankruptcy loomed on the horizon for Coleman, he shifted to new products to inject new life into the company. Inexpensive space heaters picked up some of the slack of dwindling lamp sales during the Great Depression. During World War II, the company built on an idea it had tried 20 years earlier without much success—a portable cookstove. The compact new model requested by the U.S. Army could be carried anywhere, as it weighed only three and a half pounds (1.6 kilograms). It operated on a variety of fuels in all kinds of weather, from blistering heat to subzero temperatures. One war correspondent called it and the jeep the two most important inventions to come out of the war.

A replica of the Coleman G.I. Pocket Stove manufactured during World War II

Coleman had to stay alert to keep ahead of ever-changing economic conditions. When central heating made his space heaters obsolete in the 1950s, he began to emphasize his portable cookstoves. Eventually, the camp stoves led to other

Coleman buildings occupied a large portion of this warehouse area in Wichita, Kansas, during the 1940s.

camping products, just in time to catch the growing interest in outdoor recreation.

William Coleman never did make it back to law school. Instead, he had to "settle" for starting what has since become the United States's best-known manufacturer of camping equipment.

Would You Buy
A New Car
From This Man?

Greyhound Lines

The business that was to become Greyhound Lines was started in 1913 with this Hupmobile.

GREYHOUND LINES, INC. HAS FORGED a reputation as a highly successful passenger transportation business. Yet it owes its existence to the fact that its founder was an unsuccessful car salesman. It was Carl Wickman's inability to sell even one automobile that forced him into cross-country taxi service.

Carl Eric Wickman was born in Sweden in 1887. At the age of 17, he was lured to the United States by the letters of a family friend who urged Wickman to join him in Arizona. Wickman spent his last cent on the train fare from New York City to Tucson, Arizona. But when he arrived, his friend was no longer there. Unable to speak English, Wickman found himself broke and alone in a strange land. For a while he survived by working in a sawmill.

He heard that there were Swedes working in the iron mines of northern Minnesota, and he moved there as soon as he had saved enough money.

Wickman settled in Hibbing, Minnesota, working in the mines as a diamond-drill operator. There he found companionship among the rough, hard-nosed miners, although it took many a fistfight for him to earn their respect.

Unfortunately, the mining industry was unstable. After enduring long layoffs over several years, Wickman became disenchanted. He wanted a more steady income that would enable him to settle down and start a family.

In 1913 Wickman made his career move. He purchased a dealership for Hupmobile cars and Goodyear tires. Although he had gambled correctly that automobiles were the transportation of the future, he placed his bet on the wrong car. The seven-passenger Hupmobile was simply too much car for the prospective customers in Hibbing. Although he gave demonstrations to anyone who walked by, Wickman could not get anyone even to make an offer on it.

Out of this frustration came a new idea. He would buy the car himself and try to recover the money by setting up a taxi service. He would not run it only within city limits, since another man was operating a taxi service that way. Apparently, Carl Wickman was the first person to offer transportation service from one town to another.

Many companies experience seasonal ups and downs. When business is on the upswing, they need many employees to produce all the goods that are needed. When business is on the downswing, they need fewer employees to keep up with demand. When that happens, companies **lay off**, or release, many employees from their jobs. When business improves, the companies will usually hire back the employees that were laid off before hiring any new employees.

A **dealership** is a store or other sales agency which is authorized by a company to sell its product.

Knowing miners as he did, he chose a route from Hibbing to nearby Alice, a small town in which a popular bar was located. Rates were set at 15 cents for the four-mile trip, 25 cents for a round-trip. Before long there were so many miners wanting rides that Wickman set up a regular daily schedule.

The popularity of the taxi service to Alice quickly outgrew the Hupmobile. Wickman crammed 10 passengers into the car and allowed others to stand on the running boards on the outside. But as good as business was, Wickman began to hate it. Winter was especially tough, because the car had no heater. Tires frequently went flat on the unpaved road. When that happened, passengers had to wait alongside the car as Wickman removed the flat tire, patched and reinflated it, then put it back on the car. Wickman also ran into problems trying to collect fares from passengers, and rides frequently ended in fights.

When the iron mines stepped up production because of World War I, it looked as though miners would have steady work for a long time. Wickman was happy to take his old job back. He sold the taxi business to two other Swedish immigrants, Andy Anderson and Charles Wenberg, for $1,200, twice what he had originally paid for the Hupmobile.

Unfortunately, Wenberg had never learned to drive a car, so he could hardly be trusted to drive passengers. That left all the driving to Anderson, who soon found out why Wickman had been so

Carl Wickman

eager to sell. One day, Anderson waited for Wickman outside the mine and begged him for help. If Wickman would agree to drive every other day, then the job might be tolerable for both men. Since Anderson was a friend, Wickman reluctantly agreed to get back into the taxi business. He bought back Wenberg's half of the business and alternated driving days with Anderson.

With the mines running at full capacity, miners generally had plenty of money to spend. Wickman and Anderson were busy driving the Hupmobile back and forth from Hibbing to Alice with overflow passengers riding on the running boards and clinging to the windows. Many miners used the service to get back and forth to work. In 1915 the two men made $8,000 hauling passengers in that one car. Anderson and Wickman realized the business was outgrowing the Hupmobile and began talking about getting another car. The problem was that they had not saved enough money to expand, and they didn't think that a bank would lend any to them.

At about the same time, Ralph Bogan, who ran a taxi service within the city of Hibbing, had expanded his service. After watching passengers swarm to Wickman's company, he did his competitor one better: He offered passenger service to the larger city of Duluth, 90 miles away.

Instead of viewing this as a threat to his business, Wickman saw it as an opportunity. If they could combine businesses with Bogan, they would have

Many companies realize the value of **expanding** (becoming bigger or developing different aspects of the business). Often, by expanding, a company can offer its customers more or better service. By expanding their service, Wickman and Anderson could offer more customers rides at many different times and, in the process, make the ride more comfortable for them.

Claude Graves, a driver for the Mesaba Transportation Company, stood in front of one of the company's buses. At the time, bus bodies were built on truck chassis.

A **merger** is a union of two or more companies in which one company buys another. In recent years, mergers (sometimes called takeovers) have become common.

enough resources to create a large-scale passenger service. Bogan agreed, and their two businesses merged. They took in more investors, bringing their fleet of cars and drivers to five. In 1915 they formed the Mesaba Transportation Company. Wickman managed the operation and continued to drive his usual routes.

The company adopted practices Bogan was using on the Duluth route to make traveling more comfortable. Winter passengers were provided with lap blankets and with warm bricks for their feet. Drivers were equipped with snow shovels and other equipment to pull cars out of snowbanks. But in the inhospitable climate of northern Minnesota, that was not enough. The rough, narrow roads were frequently blocked by snowdrifts. Occasionally passengers had to wade through snow in winter storms to find refuge in a farmhouse. Wickman saw no choice but to buy snowplows to keep the roads clear.

In 1917, when the United States officially entered World War I, Ralph Bogan turned his interests over to Wickman and enlisted in the army. That left Wickman in charge of an 18-car operation. Turning the driving over to employees, Wickman had more time to think about the business of transporting people from city to city.

By this time, others had begun to see the advantages of cross-country passenger service. Several automobile manufacturers took notice of the many transportation companies springing up around the country and began to tailor a line of cars for these businesses. These cars were longer and could hold more passengers than previous models. Eventually, in the 1920s, an Oakland, California, firm came out with a vehicle very much like a modern bus. Called the Safety Coach, it could seat four people in each of seven rows. Each row had its own door.

These buses became commonly known as

A 1920s bus for the Northland Transportation Company carried travelers throughout Minnesota.

A **consolidation**, in Greyhound's case, unified several bus lines under one management, or ownership.

Businesses rely on the image, or appearance, that they project to their customers. If customers have the impression that a company is more professional than another (perhaps because of its uniforms, clean buses, and reliable service), they may be more likely to do business with that company.

greyhounds, although there is disagreement as to where the nickname came from. Explanations range from the buses' long, trim appearance to their speed on the highway, and to the fact that many of them were silver in color.

At any rate, the availability of these larger vehicles contributed to the rapid growth of the bus industry. Before long the United States had been carved into a confused jumble of short bus routes, each run by a different company. Wickman saw that one way to move ahead in the industry would be to consolidate into a network of routes that would connect many major cities. That would reduce the need to buy different tickets for each stretch of travel. It would also eliminate the waiting and the luggage problems that went along with changing from one bus line to another.

In 1922 Wickman set his plan in motion. Selling all his interests in the Mesaba Transportation Company, he moved to Duluth. He used the money from his portion of the business to buy carefully selected new bus lines. Wickman attracted new customers by improving the image of the bus service. He made bus rides seem more respectable by making bus drivers wear uniforms. Whatever money his new Northland Transportation Company made was used to buy new stretches of service which were then connected to his existing ones. During one six-week period, Wickman absorbed 60 small bus lines.

During the next several years, nearly 23,000 bus companies were involved in a brutal competition for routes throughout the country. Between 1926 and 1930, nearly half of the companies went out of business. Wickman proved to be a master at acquiring bus lines and merging with others. When he ran out of money for buying bus companies, he frequently formed partnerships with other owners. By 1928 his company had forged links with every large city from Chicago and St. Louis to New York.

During the next two years, Wickman added a number of companies that had used the popular nickname "greyhound" as part of their names. When he reorganized his holdings into a new company during 1930, he chose the name The Greyhound Corporation. This Chicago-based business eventually became famous for its slogan "Leave the driving to us." Greyhound Lines, Inc. has dominated the cross-country bus transportation business since then.

The man who couldn't sell one automobile certainly found something he could sell: reliable nationwide transportation.

In the late 1930s, a celebration in Hibbing, Minnesota, featured a 1916 Greyhound bus and one of the newer buses of the time.

After Wickman bought several small bus companies, he felt they would be easier to operate as one large company. When he **reorganized** the companies, he eliminated all the smaller companies and brought them together as The Greyhound Corporation. The reorganization likely had very little affect on the services customers received, but made operation of the different routes easier for company officials to handle.

The Unbought Bank

Hilton

Conrad Hilton

AS A YOUNG BOY, CONRAD HILTON was taught to be a shrewd negotiator. From a wealth of experience in a variety of businesses, he had become very good at making business deals. But in the most important transaction of his life, Hilton let his guard down. It cost him the one thing he wanted most at the time. Fortunately for Hilton, his consolation prize was something he came to value even more.

Conrad Hilton was born in 1887 in San Antonio, New Mexico. He was the second of eight children in a family dominated by an ambitious father, Augustus Hilton. At the age of 10, Gus, as he was known to friends and family, had immigrated to the United States from Norway with his family. When Gus left home, he wound up camping with a group

51

of six others in the mountains near Socorro, in the territory of New Mexico. Gus was looking for a small town in which to start a trading store. Before he could establish a business in Socorro, however, his group was attacked by Indians. Gus was one of only two men who survived.

Eventually, Gus settled in the newly established town of San Antonio. He set up his store and kept building new businesses. Before long, he was operating nearly every business in town, including a drugstore, a general store, a post office, a bank, and a hotel.

The first Hilton hotel was actually a portion of the family house. When all of his other enterprises went through a particularly lean period in 1907, Gus squeezed his family into a small part of his large adobe house and ran the remaining five rooms as a hotel.

Young Conrad was put to work in whatever business his father needed him at the time. When the family ran its hotel, the boy was a bellhop for the Hilton inn. That task included seeking out salesmen who arrived in town by train after dark and steering them toward the family's hotel.

It was not easy working for Gus, a notoriously hard worker. Once when Conrad committed the offense of sleeping until 7:00 A.M., his father denounced him as a lazy oaf who would never amount to anything.

That prediction was quickly proved false. After

Conrad Hilton (back row, second from left) played baseball for the New Mexico School of Mines in the early 1900s.

When a business becomes, for any reason, worth less money, it has **devalued**, or gone down in value.

Negotiating is a process of reaching an agreement on some matter. Business-people will often negotiate prices of assets they wish to sell or buy. The owner will ask one price, and the potential buyer will offer a lower price. They continue the process until they can reach an agreement on a price the seller is willing to settle for and the buyer is willing to pay. Frequently, negotiations fail to come to an agreement and no deal is made.

working his way through school, Hilton entered politics. In New Mexico's first election upon becoming a state in 1912, 24-year-old Conrad Hilton won a seat in the state legislature. After serving two years, he persuaded his father to help him open a bank in San Antonio. Conrad served as the bank's cashier beginning in 1913, and by 1915 he had worked his way up to the presidency.

When the United States went to war in 1917, Hilton enlisted and was stationed in Europe. While he was away, his father died. Conrad came home to find Gus's businesses devalued, leaving $40,000 for Hilton's mother and a sister who was still living at home.

Hilton had about $5,000 saved, which he decided to use to get back into the banking business. On the advice of a friend, he headed for Texas in the summer of 1919 to find a small bank for sale. After being turned down in Wichita Falls, he tried Breckenridge with no luck. Then he found a small bank for sale farther south near the booming oil fields. In the town of Cisco, Texas, a banker was asking $75,000 for a bank Hilton felt was financially healthy. With his connections in the banking world, Hilton could easily borrow enough to close the deal.

Hilton did not haggle with the seller but offered full price. He later said it was the only time in his life he tried to close a business deal without negotiating.

The buyer, who was not in town at the time,

Just back from military duty in World War I, Conrad Hilton traveled to Cisco, Texas, in search of a bank to buy. Instead, he bought the Mobley Hotel.

interpreted Hilton's ready offer as a sign that he had priced the bank too low. Trying to get more money out of the deal, he wired back that the asking price had been raised to $80,000.

The tactic caught Hilton off guard. Irritated with both the seller for hiking up the price and himself for appearing too eager to buy, Hilton went to the Mobley Hotel to find a room. While sitting in the lobby, thinking over the latest developments with the bank, he noticed that the hotel was teeming with activity. Many more people wanted rooms than there were rooms available.

When Hilton talked with the owner about the success of his hotel, the man just shrugged. Business wasn't bad, he agreed. But what he really wanted to do was try his luck in the oil fields, where a person could make big money. If only he had the cash, he would go in a minute.

On the spur of the moment, Hilton suggested a plan that could make both of them happy. After checking the hotel's financial records, he offered to buy it. The owner agreed and settled for a price of $40,000. By the end of the day, Conrad Hilton was the owner of a 40-room hotel. It was the start of his long hotel career.

A few months later, backed as always with money from business partners, he took over another hotel in Fort Worth, Texas. In 1925 he made his first attempt at building his own hotel, the Dallas Hilton. The hotel was on the edge of bankruptcy for several years before Hilton was able to solve its financial problems.

Over the next few years, Hilton bought, sold, and built hotels until he had eight establishments under his control. But it was a poor time to be expanding in the hotel business. The Great Depression of the 1930s hit hotel operators particularly hard. More than four out of five hotels in the United States went out of business during that time. Even though he lost most of his hotels for a short while when a creditor foreclosed on him, Hilton fared better than most. When the depression was over, he had regained three of the eight hotels he had owned. But he had also run up half a million dollars in debt.

Along with timely profits from some oil lease holdings and money borrowed against his life

Conrad Hilton seldom went into a business venture without partners. Rather than finance the high cost of the hotels with his own money, he raised money through investors. After he had purchased the hotels in his own name and made them profitable, he would pay back the investors and give them additional money as a return on their investments.

Banks or other creditors usually will hold the title for a property as collateral, or guarantee, on a loan. If the borrower misses several payments or fails to repay the loan, the creditor can **foreclose** on the loan by canceling the debt and keeping the property.

insurance, Hilton's knowledge of where to pinch pennies helped him to survive the depression. Despite the shortage of money, Hilton was determined to present customers with attractive, modern rooms. Many owners of hotel chains saved money by furnishing all their hotels in the same way. Hilton insisted on each of his establishments having its own special character. Instead of scrimping on furnishings and maintenance to cut expenses, he would shut off entire floors of hotels, remove telephones, and eliminate unprofitable features such as attached cafes and restaurants.

Those hotel owners who survived the depression were able to find great bargains among the wreckage of bankruptcy. Hilton gained a reputation for acquiring large, run-down hotels at very low prices and then restoring them to top working order. One of his most useful talents was the ability to make the best use of available space. He once created thousands of feet of extra floor space by dividing an existing room in half. That task was accomplished by taking a room with an abnormally high ceiling and adding a floor midway up!

One of Hilton's biggest deals was his purchase of the prestigious Waldorf-Astoria in New York City. For a number of years, he had spoken wistfully of acquiring this 1,900-room giant hotel, which Hilton called "the greatest of them all." Yet when the opportunity came in 1949, friends tried to persuade him against buying it. The Waldorf-Astoria was

In general, an economic **depression** is a period when production and consumption of goods and services slow down. It is a time marked by unemployment and business failures, and people do not have much money to live on. During the 1930s, the United States suffered through a period called the **Great Depression**, during which the U.S. economy was paralyzed.

Conrad Hilton admired the Waldorf-Astoria in New York City. He even kept a postcard picture of the hotel on his desk. When the chance came to buy it in 1949, he took it.

Conrad Hilton, left, appeared with President Dwight Eisenhower at a National Prayer Breakfast in the 1950s.

known to be in a financial mess. Hilton would be throwing away a lot of money just for the prestige of the Waldorf-Astoria name. But Hilton made the deal and brought the hotel back to profitability.

From there, Hilton's business just kept growing. Land was purchased, and Hilton Hotels were constructed in major cities throughout the world.

With his shrewd business sense and financial wizardry, Conrad Hilton would have made his mark in the banking world. Nonetheless, it was a bank owner's attempt to wring an extra $5,000 from a sale that led Hilton to build a network of travel accommodations known throughout the world.

The Colonel's Choice

Kentucky Fried Chicken

Harland Sanders

IN 1956 COLONEL HARLAND SANDERS watched helplessly as a new interstate highway was built seven miles from his restaurant in Corbin, Kentucky. He realized that the new route would keep many potential customers from stopping at the restaurant. Without a steady stream of customers, Sanders knew he wouldn't be able keep the business running successfully.

However, the Colonel refused to concede defeat. At the age of 66, he took to the road with a secret recipe and method for making chicken. The result of this late, unplanned career change was the Kentucky Fried Chicken empire.

Harland Sanders was born on a farm near Henryville, Indiana, in 1890. His father died when Harland was only six, and his mother was forced to work long hours to support the family. She spent days peeling tomatoes in a cannery and sewed during the evenings, leaving her three children to prepare their own meals. As the oldest of the children, Harland did the cooking.

When Sanders turned 12, his mother remarried. The boy's new stepfather was not fond of children, and his mother was not sympathetic toward him. When he was in seventh grade, Sanders was taken out of school and sent to work as a farmhand in Greenwood, Indiana.

After spending a few years on the farm, 15-year-old Harland set off to make his own way in the world. For the next 25 years, Sanders tried and discarded careers as if he were trying on hats. He worked as a painter and a streetcar conductor, operated a ferryboat, sold insurance, joined the army, worked with the railroads, and earned a correspondence law degree that enabled him to become a justice of the peace in Little Rock, Arkansas.

Eventually, in 1929, Sanders ran a gas station in Corbin. He still enjoyed cooking, frequently treating his wife and children to fried chicken, his specialty. Since the family lived in the gas station's living quarters, customers could often smell the delicious aromas coming from the kitchen. After a time, Sanders began selling home-cooked meals to customers, who ate at the dining room table. More often than not, fried chicken was served.

It wasn't long before the meal portion of the

Kentucky Fried Chicken restaurants provide a service rather than a tangible good, or product. A **service** is usually used where it is produced—a restaurant meal, for example, or a haircut or a visit to the dentist.

Unlike goods, services cannot be stored. Some service industries include: health care services, such as hospitals; hotels and motels; restaurants; financial services, such as banks; and retail stores. The major goods-producing industries, on the other hand, are agriculture, manufacturing, mining, and construction.

Sanders Court and Cafe was a combination of a restaurant, gasoline station, and motel. It was one of the first establishments of its kind.

business outgrew the small family dining room. Sanders moved into a 142-seat restaurant across the street, and called it Sanders' Cafe. His fame as a chef continued to grow and in 1935 he was given the honorary title of Colonel by Kentucky Governor Ruby Laffoon. The new Colonel then went a step further and added a motel to his line of one-stop services. Sanders Court & Cafe, built long before Howard Johnson's Motor Lodges came along, was one of the first such food, fuel, and motel combinations.

Sanders tried to continue the folksy, down-home atmosphere that customers seemed to love by serving the meals family style, without a menu. But as the business grew, it became more difficult to prepare the food as quickly as customers ordered it.

Sanders solved some problems by taking a course in restaurant and hotel management at Cornell University in New York. The problem of cooking chicken quickly for so many people, however, was not so easily solved. It was always a frantic effort to prepare chicken his way before customers grew impatient.

The invention of the pressure cooker was a godsend to Colonel Sanders. It greatly reduced cooking time without burning the food. Sanders bought his first pressure cooker in 1939. After experimenting with it, he was able to cook chicken just as he liked it in less than 15 minutes. Meanwhile, he had perfected his seasoning blend of 11 herbs and spices.

At last Sanders seemed to have found his niche in life. With a fine reputation for food, and facilities large enough to accommodate droves of customers, Sanders came out of the depression years of the 1930s in great shape.

In the 1940s, his prosperity was briefly threatened. Gasoline rationing during World War II slowed his usual stream of tourists. Sanders had to close his motel because business was so poor. When the war ended, however, the Colonel reopened the motel and enjoyed a stable income for a few years.

In the early 1950s, his businesses had been appraised at about $165,000. This amount, along with his savings and monthly Social Security checks, would have guaranteed Sanders a comfortable life.

Social Security is a United States government program that provides people with a retirement income. When people work at jobs, the government takes part of their wages before they get their paychecks. When they retire from working and after they reach a certain age, the government repays them a portion of that money each month.

Auctions are sales in which people bid, or compete, against one another to buy something. A woman wanting to buy one of Sanders's ovens, for example, would tell an auctioneer how much she was willing to pay, and another person might say he would pay more. When the price reaches an amount that only one person is willing to pay, the bidding stops, and the oven is sold to the final bidder at the last price bid.

Kentucky Fried Chicken uses the slogan "We Do Chicken Right" in its advertising campaign.

Again, an outside factor threatened his security. When final plans for the new interstate highway that would cut through Kentucky were announced, it was bad news for the Colonel. The highway would bypass Corbin by several miles. The new interstate would become the favored route for tourists, who had made up Sanders's largest group of customers. Cut off from the large numbers of tourists, Sanders's business began to die off. In 1956 the Colonel auctioned his equipment to pay bills. Altogether, he received less than half of what he could have gotten for the business before the new highway was built. After his debts were cleared, Sanders's savings account was practically empty. Suddenly, Harland Sanders, the respected Kentucky Colonel, was in jeopardy of spending his final years in poverty.

Trying to find a way out of his dilemma, Sanders remembered that he had once sold his chicken recipe to a restaurant operator in Utah. The owner had done well with it, and several other people had bought Sanders's seasonings and cooking process. They usually paid Sanders five cents for every chicken sold. Now, in desperation, Sanders hoped there were others who would agree to the same deal.

With a pressure cooker and a 50-pound can of his seasoning, Sanders took to the road in a 1946 Ford to sell his secret recipe. Dressed in Southern-gentleman garb of a white suit and black string tie, the white-haired Colonel would stop at a restaurant

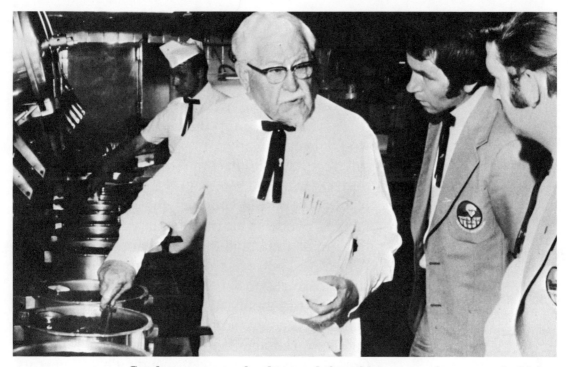

Sanders set up a school to teach franchise owners how to cook chicken exactly as he made it. Long after he sold Kentucky Fried Chicken, Sanders promoted the restaurant chain under an agreement with the new owners.

and offer to cook chicken for the owner and the staff. If they liked it, he would sell them a franchise, provide the seasoning, and teach them to cook the chicken.

At first, restaurant owners were leery of wasting their time with what appeared to be an eccentric old man. For the first two years, Sanders barely scraped by, persuading only a few owners to add his chicken to their menus. Once he finally broke through the resistance, however, his success

A **franchise** is an agreement between a company and an independently-owned dealer. The independently-owned dealer or restaurant operates as part of a chain and can use the name, product, trademark, and procedures of the company or restaurant that grants the franchise.

snowballed. By 1960 more than 200 restaurants were franchised. At the age of 70, Sanders had people clamoring to do business with him. Offers to buy franchise rights poured in, and Sanders made the restauranteurs travel to Kentucky to learn how to run a franchise.

The image of this old-time Southern Colonel serving up his Kentucky Fried Chicken intrigued reporters and television hosts. Before long Sanders's neatly trimmed white beard and mustache and black-rimmed glasses were a familiar sight throughout the country. "My mug is my trademark," he often joked.

That trademark was so effective that when Sanders sold all his franchise rights in 1964, the new owners also paid him a lifetime salary to remain as spokesman for the product. Until shortly before his death at the age of 90, Colonel Sanders traveled as many as 250,000 miles in a year promoting Kentucky Fried Chicken. He had proved not only that he could adapt to a new career at a late age, but that he could create a successful business. Kentucky Fried Chicken operates some 8,000 restaurants in 58 countries.

Kentucky Fried Chicken restaurants are all over the world.

Kentucky Fried Chicken® is a registered trademark of KFC Corporation and is used with permission.

Mary Kay Ash poses next to one of the famous pink Cadillacs the company gives its top salespeople.

Making Up for
Lost Opportunities

Mary Kay Cosmetics

Mary Kay Ash had climbed about as far up the corporate ladder as a woman was allowed in the early 1960s. But after becoming national director in charge of training sales personnel for her company, she found the path to further advancement barred. Sensing that resentment was undermining even her present position, Ash retired from the business world in 1963.

Bitter over her treatment, she took out some of her frustrations by writing down all she had learned about sales and management. Within six weeks of her retirement, she found herself wanting to get back into the business world. She decided to try selling on her own, putting into practice the things she had written down. Free to go as far as her energy and talent could take her, she formed Mary

Kay Cosmetics, a company so successful that Mary Kay became a national celebrity.

Mary Kay Wagner was born in Hot Wells, Texas, 25 miles outside of Houston. Her childhood was anything but pampered. With her father stricken by tuberculosis, Mary Kay took care of the house, while her mother worked 14-hour days managing a cafe in Houston to support the family. She was often envious of other girls who had time to enjoy their childhood.

Mary Kay became extremely competitive, which helped her to earn straight *A*s in school. She set her sights on becoming a doctor, a dream made impossible by the lack of money for college. Instead, she married a musician named Ben Rogers.

The couple had three children before Rogers was called into the armed forces during World War II. While he was away, Mary Kay took some college classes. She tried to fit in with the younger women by wearing current styles and not letting anyone know she was married. But it was difficult for her to study while she was raising three small children. Eventually, she gave it up.

Rogers returned to the United States at the end of the war, but he did not return home. The two were divorced, and Mary Kay was left with three children to support. She found work as a church secretary and then began selling cleaning products for Stanley Home Products. The techniques of selling did not come naturally to Mary Kay. During

Mary Kay (Wagner) Ash was graduated from high school with outstanding grades.

Home demonstrations are one way for salespeople to show how their products work and get people to listen to their sales pitches. Door-to-door sales are another way. Successful salespeople generally are very personable and are able to persuade their customers to buy a product from them rather than another salesperson. **Sales techniques** are ways to get customers to notice and, hopefully, buy a product or service.

Mary Kay Ash

her first three weeks of home demonstrations, she averaged sales of only seven dollars a show.

Ash's old competitiveness resurfaced, however, especially when she attended a company sales convention and saw a prize presented to Stanley's most successful saleswoman. Mary Kay was determined to achieve similar success. She took pages of notes from talking to the saleswoman and learned techniques to become a better salesperson. She learned her lessons well. Her sales increased dramatically, and she was the company's "queen of sales" the following year.

She moved on to the World Gift Company in 1953 and, within a year, she was promoted first to area manager and then to national training director.

In 1963 a consultant was hired to evaluate the company and suggest ways it could be more efficiently run. One recommendation was to cut back Ash's power. Instead of accepting new, reduced duties, Ash quit.

After writing a detailed list of problems women faced in the business world, Ash began to develop her own business plan. Her brief retirement had made her restless, so she decided to try out her ideas.

The first thing she needed was a product. For that she drew upon a memory of a party she had attended while working for Stanley Home Products. In a poor section of Dallas, she had come across a roomful of women with incredibly smooth faces.

Even some of the older women seemed unaffected by age. It turned out that the hostess had taken a solution for curing animal hides, used by her father, a tanner, and had adapted it for use as a skin-care lotion. Later, after the woman died, Ash was finally able to buy the skin-care formula from the woman's granddaughter.

Investing $5,000 of their savings, Mary Kay and her second husband rented a small, 500-square-foot storefront in Dallas and prepared to open a "Beauty by Mary Kay" store. One month before the scheduled opening of the business, her husband died. Ash was told by her financial advisers to forget

May Kay's staff in 1964 included sons Ben Rogers, second from left, and Richard Rogers, far right. Mary Kay is next to Richard.

Like all of the entrepreneurs whose stories are told in this book, Mary Kay Ash showed a willingness to take risks. A willingness to take risks is an important characteristic of people who start their own businesses. Studies have found that successful entrepreneurs often have certain other traits. These include: a strong desire to be independent; the ability to learn from experience; self-motivation; self-confidence; a lot of energy; and the willingness to work hard.

about the project. They said it was too risky and she would be out of money in a short time. At first she agreed with them, but her children and friends urged her to carry through with her plan. Defying superstition, and with the help of a son, Richard Rogers, she opened for business on Friday the 13th in September 1963. All she had to offer at the time was one shelfful of skin creams.

At first women came into the store on their lunch breaks, not to buy a product, but to get a 20-minute facial treatment. Ash quickly realized that treatments, demonstrations, makeup lessons, and beauty shows were the best ways to sell the product.

Leaving the financial aspects of the store to Richard, she began to recruit and train a sales force of women who could sell not only a product, but a complete skin-care program. One of Ash's observations over the years had been that people who just watch a demonstration are not very likely to buy the product. As a result, Mary Kay home parties were designed to get everyone in the room involved with the product.

Mary Kay also remembered when she had been a discouraged rookie salesperson for Stanley Home Products. At the convention, the company president had looked her right in the eye and told her that he believed she could accomplish whatever sales goals she set. From his encouragement, she came to appreciate the power of positive motivation and

Each year Mary Kay Cosmetics holds an awards night to present its top salespeople with awards they have earned through the company's incentive plan. In addition, crowns are awarded to "queens" in three different areas of company operations.

personal interest in employees. She was careful never to get anyone's name wrong, made certain she gave her salespeople lots of praise, and set up an incentive plan to reward their efforts. Determined not to re-create the cold business climate she had so disliked, she built flexibility into the program. Problems with home and family were given priority over job-related concerns.

Mary Kay Cosmetics earned nearly $200,000 in sales in its first year. That figure leaped to $800,000

An incentive is something that motivates people to do something, such as increase sales. Mary Kay Ash's **incentive plan** includes rewards to salespeople who sell certain amounts of Mary Kay products. By reaching certain sales goals, Mary Kay salespeople can earn diamonds, furs, or cars.

Getting cosmetics to sales-people and customers across a market area is what busi-nesspeople call distribution. **National distribution** is get-ting a product to markets all over the country. A product may go directly from the manufacturer to the con-sumer, or it may go from the manufacturer to a sales-person (or store) and then to a consumer (the person who buys the product).

by its third year. Mary Kay, who had never expected her business to expand outside the Dallas area, was already moving into national distribution by the time she married retired businessman Melvin Ash in 1966. It was as Mary Kay Ash that she grew to be almost a cult heroine among the teachers, home-makers, and secretaries who joined her company.

Her pep talks were sources of inspiration to salespeople. So were the ever more valuable incentives that came to include the famous pink Cadillacs, diamonds, minks, and luxury vacations.

By 1968 Ash was known throughout the country as simply Mary Kay. Company sales had increased to more than $10 million a year. Ten years later, her sales had reached $54 million. For Mary Kay Ash, the solution to the untimely demise of her career had been simple: She'd built a new one.

Mary Kay Cosmetics has its corpo-rate headquarters in Dallas, Texas.

For Further Reading...

Bryant, K.L., Jr. and Dethloff, H.C. *A History of American Business.* Prentice-Hall Inc., 1983.

Clary, D.C. *Great American Brands.* Fairchild Books, 1981.

Fucini, J.J. and Fucini, S. *Entrepreneurs: The Men and Women Behind Famous Brand Names.* G.K. Hall, 1985.

Livesay, H.C. *American Made: Men Who Shaped the American Economy.* Little, Brown & Company, 1980.

Moskowitz, M., Katz, M. and Levering, R., eds. *Everybody's Business.* Harper and Row, 1980.

Slappey, S.G. *Pioneers of American Business.* Grosset & Dunlap, 1970.

Sobel, R. and Sicilia, D.B. *The Entrepreneurs: An American Adventure.* Houghton Mifflin Company, 1986.

Thompson, J. *The Very Rich Book.* William Morrow & Company, 1981.

Vare, E. and Ptacek, G. *Mothers of Invention: From the Bra to the Bomb: Forgotten Women and Their Unforgettable Ideas.* William Morrow & Company, 1988.

INDEX

Words in **boldface** are defined in the text.

A

Anderson, Andy, 45-46
Armour and Company, 10
Armour, Philip, 10-11
Ash, Mary Kay, 66-73
Ash, Melvin, 73
auctions, definition of, 63

B

Baldwin, Dwight Hamilton, 9-10, 11
bankruptcy, definition of, 41
Bedell, Grace, 26
Blanchard & Kimball, 25
blue jeans, 13-21
Bogan, Ralph, 46-48
Bradley, Milton, 23-29
Burpee, Washington Atlee, 31-35
Burpee Seeds, *see* W. Atlee Burpee Co.

C

camping equipment, 37-42
Checkered Game of Life, The, 27-29
Coleman Arc Lamp, 40
Coleman Company, The, 37-42
Coleman, William C., 37-42
competition, definition of, 17
consolidation, definition of, 49
Cooper College, 40
Cornell University, 62
corporation, definition of, 21

D

Dallas Hilton, 55

Davis, Jacob, 15-18, 21
dealership, definition of, 44
debt, definition of, 41
denim, 18
depression, definition of, 56
devalue, definition of, 53
development, *see* research and
    development
distributing company, definition of, 39

E

expansion, definition of, 46

F

Fairmont College (Wichita State), 40
foreclose, definition of, 55
franchise, definition of, 64

G

games, 23-29
gasoline lanterns, 37-42
Goodyear tires, 44
Great Depression, definition of, 56;
    41, 55-56, 62
Greyhound Corporation, The, 50
Greyhound Lines, Inc., 43-50

H

Hilton, Augustus (Gus), 51-53
Hilton, Conrad, 51-58
Hilton hotels, 11, 51-58
home demonstration, definition of, 69

Howard Johnson Motor Lodges, 61
Hupmobile (car), 43, 44, 45, 46

I

incentive plan, definition of, 72
investment, definition of, 23

K

Kentucky Fried Chicken, 11, 59-65

L

Laffoon, Governor Ruby (Kentucky), 61
Lawrence Scientific School, 25
layoff, definition of, 44
Levi Strauss & Co., 11, 13-21
Lincoln, Abraham, 23, 25-26

M

mail-order business, definition of, 33
Mansion of Happiness, The, 27-29
manufacture, definition of, 23
Mary Kay Cosmetics, 67-73
merger, definition of, 47
Mesaba Transportation Company, 47, 49
Milton Bradley & Company, 29
Milton Bradley Company, 23-29
Mobley Hotel, 54-55

N

national distribution, definition of, 73
negotiating, definition of, 53
Northland Transportation Company, 49

P

partnership, definition of, 21

patent, definition of, 18
patent rights, definition of, 40
premium, definition of, 33
production costs, definition of, 20
product lines, definition of, 29
proprietorship, *see* sole proprietorship

R

reorganization, definition of, 50
research and development, definition of, 34
Rogers, Ben, 70
Rogers, Richard, 70, 71
Roosevelt, President Franklin, 41

S

Safety Coach, 48
sales techniques, definition of, 69
sales territories, definition of, 39
Sanders' Cafe, 61
Sanders, Colonel Harland, 59-65
Sanders Court & Cafe, 61
service, definition of, 60
Simmons, Zalmon, 10-11
Social Security, definition of, 62
sole proprietorship, definition of, 21
Stanley Home Products, 68, 70, 71
Stern, David, 14, 15
Strauss, Levi, 13-21; *see also*
    Levi Strauss & Co.

T

trade journals, definition of, 32
trademark, definition of, 18

U

University of Kansas School of Law, 38

University of Pennsylvania, 32
U.S. Army, 41

W

W. Atlee Burpee Co., 31-35
Wagner, Mary Kay, *see* Ash, Mary Kay
Waldorf-Astoria, 56-58
Wenberg, Charles, 45, 46
Wichita State, *see* Fairmont College
Wickman, Carl, 43-50
World Gift Company, 69
World War I, 20, 45, 48, 53
World War II, 41, 62, 68

ACKNOWLEDGEMENTS

The photographs and illustrations in this book are reproduced through the courtesy of: pp. 1, 12, 15 (all), 16, 18, 19, 20, Levi Strauss & Co.; 2, 30 (both), 31, 33, 34, 35, W. Atlee Burpee & Co.; 8, 9, Baldwin Piano & Organ Company; 10 (both), Armour and Company; 11, Simmons Company; 22, 24, 27, 28 (all), 29, Milton Bradley Company Subsidiary of Hasbro, Inc.; 26 (left), George Peter Alexander Healy/ABRAHAM LINCOLN In the collection of The Corcoran Gallery of Art, Museum Purchase, Gallery Fund; 26 (right), Dictionary of American Portraits; 36, 39, 40, 41 (both), 42, The Coleman Company, Inc.; 43, 44, 47, 49, 50, Hibbing (Minnesota) Historical Society; 51, 53, 54, 57, 58, Hilton Hotels Corporation; 59, 61, 63, 64, 65, 78, KFC Corporation; 66, Don Netzer/Mary Kay Cosmetics, Inc.; 68, 69, 70, 72, 73, Mary Kay Cosmetics, Inc.

Cover illustration by Stephen Clement.

Life® Stratego® Chutes and Ladders® Candyland® Battleship® and Twister® are registered trademarks. Permission for use granted by Milton Bradley Company Subsidiary of Hasbro, Inc.

About the Author

Nathan Aaseng is a full-time writer who has had many books published in the areas of biography, nature, sports strategy, and fiction. He grew up in Minneapolis, Minnesota, and was graduated from Luther College in Decorah, Iowa. He lives in Eau Claire, Wisconsin, with his wife and four children.

Read more about the business world in these Lerner books by Nathan Aaseng:

Better Mousetraps
Product Improvements That Led to Success

Close Calls
From the Brink of Ruin to Business Success

★The Fortunate Fortunes
Business Successes That Began With a Lucky Break

★The Problem Solvers
People Who Turned Problems into Products

From Rags to Riches
People Who Started Businesses from Scratch

★The Rejects
People and Products That Outsmarted the Experts

★The Unsung Heroes
Unheralded People Who Invented Famous Products

In its starred review of the first four books in this series, *Booklist* said:
★*"Aaseng gives captivating examples of exceptional marketing techniques in this quartet of titles…"*